Piano · Vocal · Guitar

The Kara DioGuardi Songbook

ISBN 978-1-4234-7350-3

HAL•LEONARD®
CORPORATION

7777 W. BLUEMOUND RD. P.O. BOX 13819 MILWAUKEE, WI 53213

Visit Hal Leonard Online at
www.halleonard.com

As a songwriter, you dream of hearing your music on the radio. I still cherish that first moment, driving with my brother to visit my grandmother, when I heard "Escape" (my first U.S. hit) on the radio. I have been fortunate to work with some of my industry's most talented artists, like Pink, Christina Aguilera, and Kelly Clarkson. I would like to thank all the people involved in these songs, for enabling my melodies and lyrics to reach millions of people. For that I am eternally grateful to each and every one of them. I am also thankful for every first kiss, heart break, and emotional experience in my life that moved me to a place where I could express myself.

As you read this book, it is my hope that the words and music strike a chord within you. "Ain't No Other Man" and "Pieces of Me" celebrate the healing power of love. "Taking Chances" is meant to encourage you to think outside the box and follow your heart, no matter how hard it may be. "Walk Away" is about finding strength within yourself to leave with your pride and dignity intact. "I Don't Need a Man" encourages young women to create their own identity and persona, independent from people they love. "Sober" reminds us to keep our vices in check and that our true self is beautiful. Each song has a message. A message from me to you.

I hope that you find something in your life that you love to do. Thanks to music, I have.

Kara

March, 2009

AIN'T NO OTHER MAN

Words and Music by CHRISTINA AGUILERA,
KARA DioGUARDI, CHRIS MARTIN,
CHARLES ROANE and HAROLD BEATTY

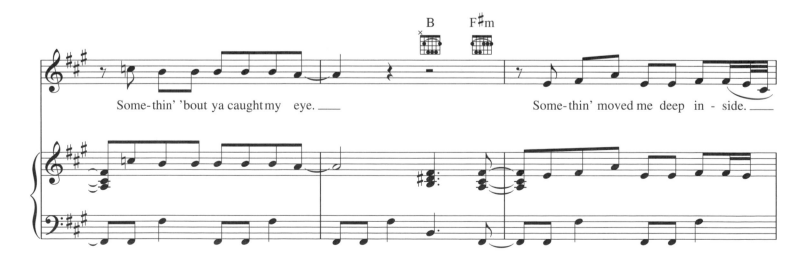

13

BABY LOVE

Words and Music by NICOLE SCHERZINGER, KARA DioGUARDI,
WILL ADAMS and KEITH HARRIS

* Recorded a half step lower.

BEEP

Words and Music by JEFF LYNNE,
KARA DioGUARDI and WILL ADAMS

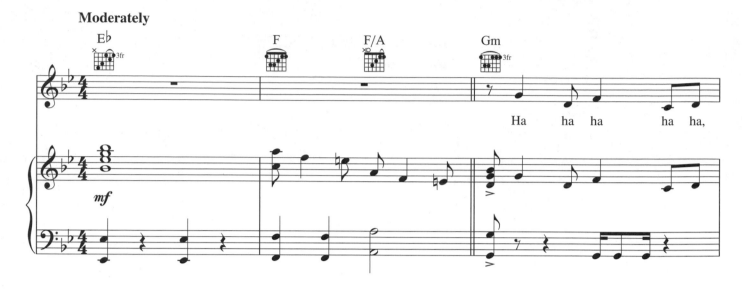

Moderately

Ha ha ha ha ha,

ha ha ha ha ha. Ha ha ha ha ha ha ha ha ha. It's

fun-ny how a man on-ly thinks a-bout the... You got a real big heart, but I'm look-ing at your... You got

COME CLEAN

Words and Music by KARA DioGUARDI
and JOHN SHANKS

Moderately

Let's go ___ back, ___

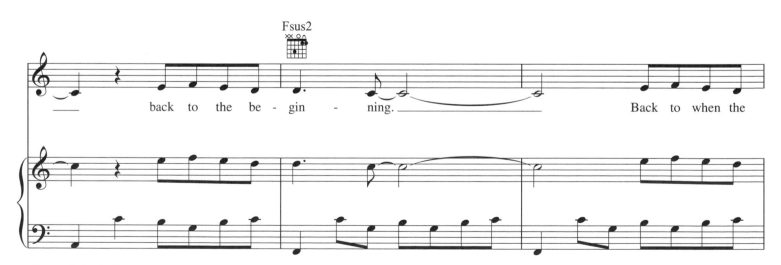

___ back to the be - gin - ning. ___ Back to when the

Recorded a half step lower.

DON'T TURN OFF THE LIGHTS

Words and Music by ENRIQUE IGLESIAS,
DAVID SIEGEL, STEVE MORALES
and KARA DioGUARDI

Lyrics:

I don't have to tell you what this is all a-bout 'cause, ba-by, half the fun is in us fig-ur-ing it all out.

ESCAPE

Words and Music by ENRIQUE IGLESIAS,
DAVID SIEGEL, STEVE MORALES
and KARA DioGUARDI

Recorded a half step higher.

FIRST

Written by KARA DioGUARDI
and JOHN SHANKS

I LUV BEING A GIRL

Words and Music by KARA DioGUARDI,
NICLAS MOLINDER and JOACIM PERSSON

Moderately fast

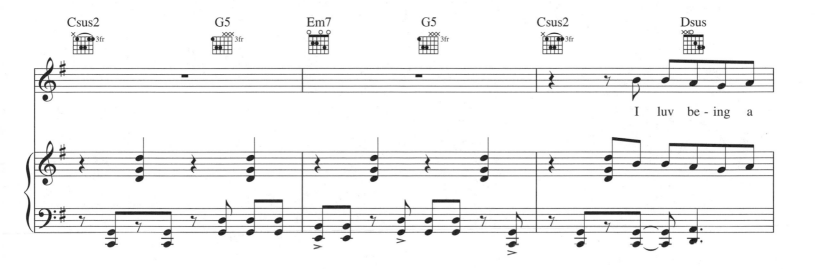

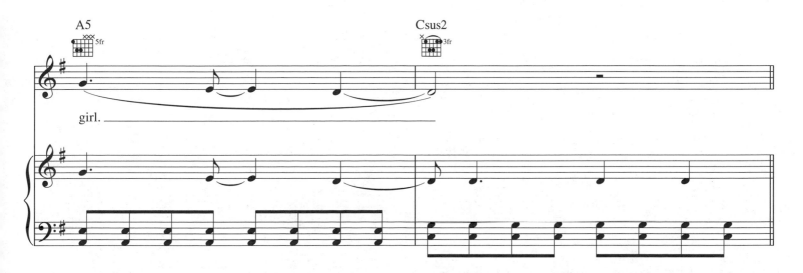

I DON'T NEED A MAN

Words and Music by RICH HARRISON, VANESSA BROWN,
KARA DioGUARDI and NICOLE SCHERZINGER

I see you

look-ing at me like I got some-thing that's for _____ you. And the
got my own life, and I bought ev-'ry-thing that's in _____ it, so if you

way that you stare, don't you dare, 'cause I'm not a-bout _____ to just give it
wan-na be with me, it ain't all a-bout the bling you're bring - in'. I want a

You know, I've

LALA

Words and Music by ASHLEE SIMPSON,
JOHN SHANKS and KARA DioGUARDI

L.O.V.E.

Words and Music by ASHLEE SIMPSON,
JOHN SHANKS and KARA DioGUARDI

Moderate Pop

I'm talk - in' 'bout love.

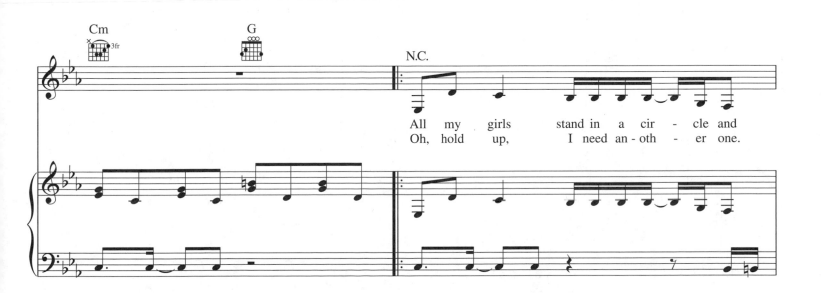

All my girls   stand in a cir - cle and
Oh, hold up,   I need an - oth - er one.

clap your hands, this is for you. Ups and downs, highs and lows and no
I think you, you do too. Grab my bag, got my own mon - ey. Don't

mat - ter what you see me through. My boy-friend he don't an - swer on the tel - e - phone.
Need an - y man in this room. My boy-friend he'll be call - in' me now an - y - time.

I don't e - ven know where the hell he goes. But all my girls, we're in a cir - cle and
I need all my girls to keep him off my mind. So hold up, we need an - oth - er one.

no - bod - y's gon - na break through.
What we got is all good.

L, O, L, O, L, O, L O V E,

PIECES OF ME

Words and Music by ASHLEE SIMPSON,
JOHN SHANKS and KARA DioGUARDI

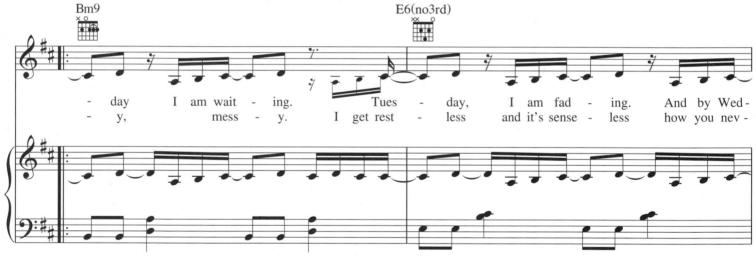

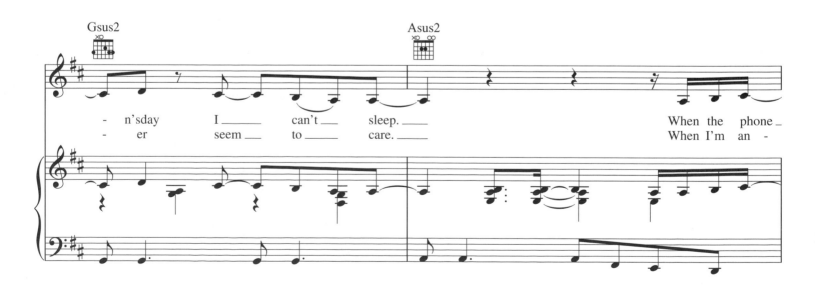

PLAY MY MUSIC

from the Disney Channel Original Movie CAMP ROCK

Words and Music by KARA DioGUARDI
and MITCH ALLAN

RICH GIRL

Words and Music by MICHAEL ELIZONDO, EVE JEFFERS, CHANTAL KREVIAZUK,
ANDRE YOUNG, GWEN STEFANI, KARA DioGUARDI,
MARK BATSON, SHELDON HARNICK and JERRY BOCK

CODA I

D.S. al Coda I

hur - ry up and come and save me.

Come to - geth - er all o - ver the world. __ From the

hoods of Jap - an, Har - a - ju - ku girls. __ What? It's all love. What? Give it up. What? Should - n't

1

mat - ter. Should - n't mat - ter. Should - n't mat - ter. Should - n't mat - ter. What?

2

mat - ter. Should - n't mat - ter. Should - n't mat - ter. Should - n't mat - ter. What

climbed all the way from the bot-tom to the top now we ain't get-tin' noth-in' but love.

CODA II

C5

girl. _____ Na, na,__ na, na, na, na, na, na,__ na, na, na, na,

na, na,__ na, na, na,__ na na, na,__ na, na. Na, na, na, na,__ na, na, na, na,

na, na,__ na, na, na, na, na, na,__ na, na, na,__ na, na, na,__ na, na.

SOBER

Words and Music by ALECIA MOORE,
KARA DioGUARDI, NATHANIEL HILLS
and MARCELLA ARAICA

Pop Rock

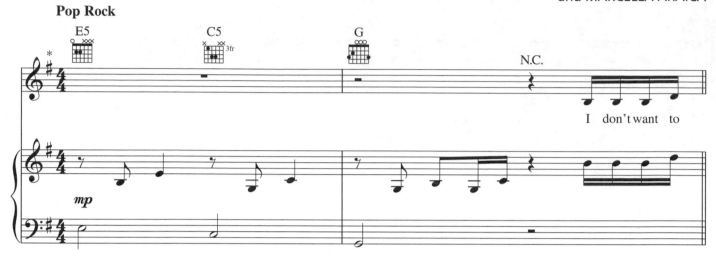

I don't want to

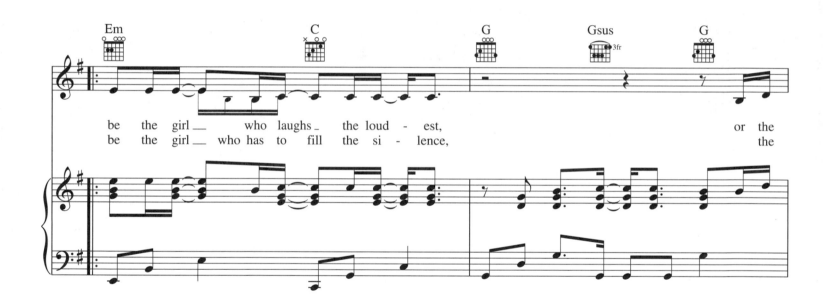

be the girl ___ who laughs ___ the loud- est,
be the girl ___ who has to fill the si - lence,

or the
the

girl who nev- er wants to be ___ a - lone. ___
qui- et scares me 'cause it screams ___ the truth. ___

I don't want to
Please ___ don't ___

Recorded a half step lower.

SPINNING AROUND

Words and Music by PAULA ABDUL, KARA DioGUARDI,
IRA SCHICKMAN and OSBORNE BINGHAM

119

SOMEBODY'S ME

Words and Music by KARA DioGUARDI
ENRIQUE IGLESIAS and JOHN SHANKS

D.S. al Coda
(take 3rd ending)

that some-bod-y's me. ___

CODA

You will al - ways be in my ___ life, e - ven

if I'm not in your ___ life, 'cause you're in my mem - o - ry. ___

You, when you re - mem - ber me, ___

TAKING CHANCES

Words and Music by DAVE STEWART
and KARA DioGUARDI

WALK AWAY

Words and Music by KELLY CLARKSON,
CHANTAL KREVIAZUK, RAINE MAIDA
and KARA DioGUARDI